Making Room for Christmas

Preparing a Place for the Christ Child

HERBERT BROKERING

Augsburg

MINNEAPOLIS

To my wife Lois
for opening doors to rooms of compassion

MAKING ROOM FOR CHRISTMAS
Preparing a Place for the Christ Child

Large-quantity purchases or custom editions of this book are available at a discount from the publisher. For more information, contact the sales department at Augsburg Fortress, Publishers, 1-800-328-4648, or write to: Sales Director, Augsburg Fortress, Publishers, P.O. Box 1209, Minneapolis, MN 55440-1209.

Cover art copyright © 2001 Banco de México Diego Rivera and Frida Kahlo Museums Trust. Av. Cinco de Mayo No. 2, Col. Centro, Del. Cuauhtémoc, 06059, México, D.F. Used by permission.

Cover design: Craig Claeys
Interior design: Marti Naughton

ISBN: 0-8066-4145-2

The paper used in this publication meets the minimum requirements of American National Standard for Information Sciences—Permanence of Paper for Printed Library Materials, ANSI Z329.48-1984. ♾ ™

Manufactured in the U.S.A. AF 9-4145

05   04   03   02   01   1   2   3   4   5   6   7   8   9   10

CONTENTS

Welcome to Christmas!		5
DECEMBER 1	*House of Memories*	8
DECEMBER 2	*House of Silence*	10
DECEMBER 3	*Farm House*	12
DECEMBER 4	*Garden of Solitude*	14
DECEMBER 5	*House of Sadness*	16
DECEMBER 6	*Children at Prayer*	18
DECEMBER 7	*Dysfunctional Family*	20
DECEMBER 8	*Halfway House*	22
DECEMBER 9	*Nursing Home*	24
DECEMBER 10	*Birthday Party*	26
DECEMBER 11	*House of Mourning*	28
DECEMBER 12	*Army Barracks*	30
DECEMBER 13	*Food Shelter*	32
DECEMBER 14	*Five-Star Hotel*	34
DECEMBER 15	*Boarding House*	36
DECEMBER 16	*Family Meal*	38
DECEMBER 17	*Prison*	40
DECEMBER 18	*Day Care Center*	42
DECEMBER 19	*House of Loss*	44
DECEMBER 20	*Wedding Reception*	46

DECEMBER 21	*Bible Study*	*48*
DECEMBER 22	*Tavern*	*50*
DECEMBER 23	*Bus Depot*	*52*
DECEMBER 24	*Department Store*	*54*
DECEMBER 25	*Intensive Care Unit*	*56*
DECEMBER 26	*House of Anger*	*58*
DECEMBER 27	*Airport*	*60*
DECEMBER 28	*Family Devotions*	*62*
DECEMBER 29	*Home Communion*	*64*
DECEMBER 30	*Refugee Camp*	*66*
DECEMBER 31	*New Year's Watch*	*68*
JANUARY 1	*New Year's Party*	*70*
JANUARY 2	*Battlefield*	*72*
JANUARY 3	*Governor's Mansion*	*74*
JANUARY 4	*House of Stars and Lights*	*76*
JANUARY 5	*Revival Tent*	*78*
JANUARY 6	*Spring and Oak*	*80*

Welcome to Christmas!

M *aking Room for Christmas* is a collection of dialogues that recall Mary and Joseph's search for lodging in Bethlehem. This Christmas "journey" is patterned after the wonderful Latin American tradition of *Las Posadas*—Spanish for "the inns"—in which villagers reenact the Holy Couple's search for an inn or shelter where the Holy Child can be born.

Tradition has it that Mary and Joseph traveled for nine days before finally being welcomed into a shelter. And so, beginning on December 16, candlelit processions set out through towns and villages, carrying figures of Mary and Joseph to prearranged homes. At each house, the procession knocks at the door entreating lodging: "In the name of Heaven, I beg you for lodging." The first responses are not welcoming: "This is not an inn, so keep going . . . don't bother us." The exchanges continue until, at last, the couple is invited inside. Then the evening ends with singing, dancing, and celebration. Finally, on the final night, Christmas Eve, the procession moves to the local church or cathedral, where the entire village welcomes the Holy Couple with a service of joy and thanksgiving as the Holy Child is born once again.

This book borrows the framework of *Las Posadas* to present a series of Advent and Christmas meditations. Each reflection offers a glimpse of Mary and Joseph at the door of a home, asking for lodging. Each reflection also asks the *readers*: "Is there room here—in your home, in your heart—for the Christ child to be born?" There are thirty-seven meditations—one for each day in December and for the first six days of January—moving readers through Advent and Christmas and ending with the festival of Epiphany.

In each reflection, Mary and Joseph are welcomed inside—but only after a dialogue in which the heart is opened or closed to the Christ child. The "houses" in these meditations represent universal situations and experiences—hearts and homes of the poor, the aged or infirm, prisoners, families who are splintered or hurting, sick and dying persons, celebrants, joyous and rejoicing homes—places where Christ seeks entrance in the Christmas season and always.

The meditations lend themselves to quiet, introspective reading by individuals or to dramatic dialogues by couples who alternate reading the lines (words of Mary or Joseph are written in italic). Or they may be read by whole families and groups of friends who, as in the tradition of *Las Posadas*, alternate homes or settings for the readings and conclude each evening with Advent or Christmas celebrations: sharing food and drink, singing songs and praying, wrapping gifts, writing Christmas cards, making and breaking piñatas, planning and executing works of kindness or charity.

Here are additional suggestions that can help enrich these evenings of meditation and reflection.

- To help create a mood and focus for the readings, begin by lighting a candle (or Advent wreath) and reciting, as an invocation, this entreaty—printed at the beginning of each reading:

  We need a room, we saw the light.
  Will you make us a room for just tonight?

- Close the meditations with Mary's song of praise, *Magnificat*. Use the words here, or choose another version of Luke 1:46b–55.

  My soul doth magnify the Lord, And my spirit hath rejoiced in God my Saviour. For he hath regarded the low estate of his handmaiden:

for, behold, from henceforth all generations shall call me blessed. For he that is mighty hath done to me great things; and holy is his name.

And his mercy is on them that fear him from generation to generation. He hath shown strength with his arm; he hath scattered the proud in the imagination of their hearts. He hath put down the mighty from their seats, and exalted them of low degree. He hath filled the hungry with good things; and the rich he hath sent empty away. He hath helped his servant Israel, in remembrance of his mercy; as he spake to our fathers, to Abraham, and to his seed forever. (KJV)

Blessings as you welcome the Christ child into your own heart and home this Christmas season.

House of Memories

WE NEED A ROOM, WE SAW THE LIGHT.
WILL YOU MAKE US A ROOM FOR JUST TONIGHT?

Thank you for opening the door. We are in need of a room for overnight. It's been a long trip and Mary needs a place to rest. She is pregnant, as you see. I am Joseph.

We've lived here for many years. We cannot move as quickly as we used to.

You have many souvenirs.

We dust them often. We know stories about each piece.

Our life together is not so old. In fact, our story is just beginning. The child who is coming will give us something new to think of. It can be the same for you.

Children grow older. They leave and leave things behind. We saved their things. But now they do not want them, we cannot give them away. And these things are all that are left to us.

Mary's child will give us all a future. If Mary can birth a child in this house you would have someone to follow into the future. He will take you into the years ahead.

We may not have many years, not as many as those behind us.

This child will take you further into the future than years. This child will take you on a way that has no end.

Our life has been good and long.

The life to be born tonight is longer than years, a life that will not end.

We have written our will and listed what is to be given away. We want most of it to go to those who know us. Perhaps they can let these things go.

The child will show you other things that are yours: treasures stored in your hearts and minds, the hopes and dreams that will come true for you.

The child knows these things? Then the child is like a prophet.

When the child is born here, you will find a treasure inside you. There are many rooms this child will show you. One of the rooms in you is the room of remembrance.

We know that room well. We've lived in it for a long time.

The child will show you memories that only believers know. The child will make you glad in ways you have never known.

Oh yes, the mother and child are welcome here. We have a guest room filled with pictures of family members who have gone ahead. There the child can be born on an old bed from years ago, in the middle of portraits of family. Our "saints," we call them.

The child knows of saints. The child just came from where they live, and will take you there.

That is why we keep so many of these treasures, these memories. They take us down memory lane.

The way that begins at the end of memory lane. The child is the Lord.

Here is the room.

This is the house of the Lord. For sure. "For sure" means Amen.

Dear God, take us on the Way with you.

House of Silence

WE NEED A ROOM, WE SAW THE LIGHT.
WILL YOU MAKE US A ROOM FOR JUST TONIGHT?

Thank you for answering the door. It was so quiet we didn't know anyone was home. This is Mary; she is pregnant, as you can tell. I am Joseph. We are looking for a gentle place for her to give birth tonight.

So you are looking for shelter here?

Just a quiet bed to give birth.

Well, it is quiet here. My parents haven't talked with me for days—longer it seems. At least, not in a way that feels like conversation. We're not on speaking or listening terms.

You're young. Was it something you did that caused this silence, or something they did?

We blame each other. It's things we say and don't say, things we do and don't do for each other.

Do you have room for us?

We have room. I don't stay here full-time. I stay with friends, or in places that feel better than my own home feels. You could have my room, if you don't mind things lying around. I can stay anywhere.

What will the others say?

They don't need to know. I doubt if they'd care. They're out; I don't know where, and I don't know when they'll be back.

What will they think if they come home and find a child being born in this house?

It might give us something to talk about. It might make us talk again. We need something like this to happen here. Something really different. I'd like something alive and new to happen in this place.

This birth will give you something to talk about, something alive and new. This birth will be special. The child will be special. We are calling him Jesus.

I know about Jesus, but I don't know anyone named Jesus.

Soon you will. You will know the child who is Jesus. But the baby will cry when he is born; the house will not be quiet anymore.

He'll probably cry a lot after he's born, too. We sure do around here. At least I do. Sometimes it gets too quiet even to cry.

Where will you sleep tonight?

I'll put a pillow near the doorway. When the others come home, I'll tell them what's happening. It'll give me something important to say to them.

It's a very new thing that is happening. Something that needs talking about. Something that can help you talk.

I'm ready for something really new to happen, something to talk about.

Dear God, let us talk about you—together.

Farm House

WE NEED A ROOM, WE SAW THE LIGHT.
WILL YOU MAKE US A ROOM FOR JUST TONIGHT?

You came so suddenly, as though you're expecting company. Mary needs a place to rest. You see that she is with child. I am Joseph. We noticed your open door.

In this season we are always ready for company, often unexpected. Someone always comes. Sometimes from nearby, sometimes from far away.

We came far, from Nazareth in Galilee. This region is our destination. We must find a room for this night.

We've never had anyone travel so far to get here. You must need a shower, clean clothes, food. And your wife needs a place to lie down. You seem to be traveling light. Can you repeat your names?

Mary and Joseph. The child will be born tonight. He will be named Jesus.

A good name. It's important what you name a kid. We gave our children names that had meaning for us.

Jesus means "savior." He will save towns and nations and farms and families. That is the promise an angel gave Mary. She believes the angel; so do I.

As you can notice we have lots of angel pictures around. There's this angel music box the children have all played.

The child will have angels on every side. We believe angels know about this child, this birth. They will sing when he is born.

We believe angels sing for special occasions. Never thought of an angel choir in our house singing an anthem. You are welcome to stay. We never know who's going to drop in.

There's a lot we don't know beforehand. Your door is a door we did not know was open. We can stay here tonight. We can be your company.

We wouldn't have it any other way. Sometimes you resent company that drops in unannounced. But when they leave, you miss them.

When we leave, be sure to stay in touch with the child. In that way we can be part of each other's family.

That's what strangers can get to be—family. Real close family. We have people drop in who stay more connected to us than family.

The child will always be easy to find. That is a promise of God. And if you find this child, you will find a very large family.

We like the idea of one big happy family in the world.

It won't always be a happy family. But it will be big, and it will be one family. The child is being born to bring the family together again, to make its members happy. The angel told his mother that his kingdom, his family, will have no end.

That sounds good to us. Come in, come in. We'll give you a room that's full of color—paintings of children playing under rainbows, holding hands, hugging and kissing. We fixed it up for our own children. And when you're settled, we've got a big meal to share.

When Jesus is older, we will tell him stories of rainbows and this place. Thank you. How quickly strangers become family.

Dear God, turn strangers into family.

Garden of Solitude

WE NEED A ROOM, WE SAW THE LIGHT.
WILL YOU MAKE US A ROOM FOR JUST TONIGHT?

I am sorry to interrupt your work. Your garden is so lovely with the flowers in full bloom.

Is there something you need? The sun will set soon.

We need your help. My name is Mary and I am with child. Joseph and I need a place for a birth tonight.

I'm not sure this is a place to begin a new life. We live here together, but each of us is alone. Not a good home for a birth.

It looks like a good place. Well kept.

The place is not the problem. That's not what's breaking apart.

The child inside me will bring it together. He will heal broken-hearted lives. I learned this from a song of my ancestors.

I think it's too late. I work outside as long as I can. I bury my feelings in the earth. Flowers are the only things I can grow that give me hope.

His name will be Hope. He will give hope, reconcile, connect. Some will call him Seed, Root, Stem. Beginnings, growth.

Strange names for a kid. Seed, Root, Stem. All about beginnings, life, growth.

The child will always be about beginnings. Through him, we will all be tied to Beginning, to Alpha.

What is Alpha?

God. The Creator. The One who gives life. Grows gardens, seeds, blossoms.

So the child is about beginnings. About God?

And endings. He also will be known as End, Omega. Omega is life beyond this time. Beyond the end. These are both inside the child. Inside every mother's baby. We all have this in common: beginnings and endings.

I'm afraid we have lost what we had in common. I feel only endings. The end of connection, the end of love, of our life together.

Then comes Beginning. There is much you have together. What connects you is in the child.

How can the child save us in this one night? We are a broken home.

The child is like a seed that brings new life. The child alive inside me also can live inside you.

I want this child. It will be an honor to have him born in this place tonight. Here's a rose for you, Mary. I will listen for his birth cry.

When you hear the child's birth cry, listen for your own birth cry. That is how life begins, with a cry. And then there is laughter. Sometimes there's a lot of crying. Then, laughter. Tonight you will hear both: crying and laughter.

How long will the laughter last?

Into the end. We cry and we laugh from beginning to end. The child will lead us.

*Dear God, show us the seeds of endings and beginnings
inside ourselves.*

DECEMBER 5
House of Sadness

WE NEED A ROOM, WE SAW THE LIGHT.
WILL YOU MAKE US A ROOM FOR JUST TONIGHT?

It took you long to answer the door. We are sorry to bother you. I am Joseph. Mary is with child and needs a good rest.

I am on medication, which makes me very tired.

Mary's child will be born to make people well. That is the promise.

So he'll be a doctor someday? I have good doctors—three of them, each for a different thing. But I still feel sad a lot and alone. I am all alone, you see.

We can be your family. We can be like a family doctor. Together we will not be alone.

What will you name the child?

Immanuel. The name means God is with us.

I believe in God. I read the Bible. But I am often very sad. Perhaps it is the medicine that does it. I don't know, it's been with me so long, this sadness.

Immanuel will make people glad. Songs of joy and praise will be written about him. Already there are songs of praise that mention him. They are in the book of Psalms.

I read that book. Some of the songs are very sad. They talk about fear, about worry. They talk to God about those feelings. I read the songs out loud. That helps.

Singing gets the worry out, helps the ones singing to see the praise inside themselves. The singer finds medicine: relief, healing, joy. Praise.

Immanuel songs are medicine?

Deep inside the brain are enzymes that fill our bodies when we laugh and sing and praise. There is a medicine in us that Immanuel stirs up.

You are faith healers.

Faith in Immanuel heals. This is the best medicine. Immanuel gives us faith and healing.

Is that why you came here, to tell me this?

We came here in order for Immanuel to be born in this place.

Would my doctors approve?

Doctors know this medicine. They know where all medicine begins.

The pharmaceutical factories?

A higher factory. The factory in your mind, where wellness is manufactured. Healing can happen with medicine from the pharmacy, it can happen by singing, praying. But all medicine is about Immanuel, God with us.

I want that medicine. You can have my bedroom for the birth. It's where I spend a lot of time. It's where I read the song of psalms each day. I will sleep where I often do, the easy chair.

If you hear Mary singing it will be a medicine song.

I will be in the next room, listening.

Dear God, praise will heal sadness.

Children at Prayer

WE NEED A ROOM, WE SAW THE LIGHT.
WILL YOU MAKE US A ROOM FOR JUST TONIGHT?

Is this a good time to ask for help? The sun is down, and we see by the toys in your yard that you have children. I am Joseph. Mary, here, is with child. We need lodging.

I'll want to ask my wife. Our children are in bed saying their prayers and she's with them, listening. It usually takes awhile. You know how children pray for everything.

There's a lot to pray for. Children seem to know.

They pray for everyone they know. Prayer also makes the day go on a little while longer, postpones sleep and night. The children like these between-times: the end of today and the beginning of tomorrow. And they like being with one of us—their mother or me—during these between-times. I'm sorry, I forgot my manners. Please come in.

Thank you. We are here between times. Mary's child will be called Jesus. He will be the end of what was and the beginning of what will be.

That's an important way to see a child, as a kind of bridge between yesterday and tomorrow. It looks like you have been traveling for some time. How far have you come?

The child came from Heaven. Jesus, the child in Mary, is the Son of God. He has been coming since the beginning of time. When he is born, a new time will begin.

One child can make a huge difference in the world. I hope one of our children will make a difference for good.

Our child's name—Jesus—tells what he will do, the difference he will make. He will save the hearts of the people.

Our children love to sing the prayer, "Come into My Heart." They think of their heart as a room inside themselves.

That is the room we are looking for. Not just a place for Mary to give birth, but hearts that remember the birth, hearts that hold Jesus on the inside, to share him on the outside.

Our children have good imaginations. They can imagine someone being born in their hearts. Perhaps I can bring you to where they are praying? They will have many questions for you.

You said they like to sing a prayer. When they are finished asking Mary and me their questions, we will hear their song. They may place their hands against the child and sing. It will make the baby happy. Their hearts will give us all pleasure.

Come, then. I know they will be happy you are naming your child Jesus. When we pray, we always finish with this name: Jesus.

When they have sung to the child, Mary can sing her song about the child. The music will quiet your children. Then we will leave the room.

But not our home. We have a room for you. Stay, please, and be our guests. It will bless our home.

Perhaps, then, in the morning Mary will sing her song once more, while your children hold the baby in their hearts.

Dear God, make room in our hearts.

DECEMBER 7
Dysfunctional Family

I think we've come at a bad time. You seem troubled.

It's this way a lot. Someone is always getting angry or bossy or blaming. This has been going on for years.

I am Mary, this is Joseph. The child in me will be named Jesus.

Jesus. That word sure gets used in this family a lot. And that's going to be his name? Jesus?

Yes, it's a name God gave us. A holy name. And he will do what the name means.

In this marriage "Jesus" means get mad, yell, tell someone off.

That is not what God meant for the name. Jesus means one who will save people from anger, hurt, blame.

I know. I know: we're using the word wrong. But we sure know the name. You didn't come to talk about our problems. Why are you here?

We need a place to stay, a place for me to give birth to Jesus—tonight. He will bring peace to a needy world.

We're a needy family. Seems to me like this is the exact place for him to be born. Maybe it's true that there are no accidents. We need this kind of Jesus that you're talking about.

He will be called the Prince of Peace.

We can keep him busy full time, right here. I don't know if you'll like the place we can offer you. Our house doesn't have such a good reputation. We've been known to disturb the neighbors. The police have been by a lot of nights. The fighting mostly happens at night, when we're alone together.

This is a good place for my son. He will bring healing and peace. He will bring forgiveness.

Forgiveness, huh? I guess we don't even know what that means here. We've said "I'm sorry" so often the words don't mean anything. One more time makes no difference; no one believes it. When you really are sorry and no one believes you, that hurts the most.

Forgiveness doesn't keep count. There's always one more time. That's what God told us about the child in me. The child will not keep track of how often to forgive.

That's a lot of forgiveness. It's hard to picture.

It's endless. Higher, deeper, wider, and longer than anything we know. That's the kind of love God has, the kind of forgiveness God offers. And the child will prove it.

We can use endless healing in this place. Maybe having you overnight will make a difference. Are you sure you won't mind if things get out of control?

God told us about the world Jesus will make well. It is why he has come. We will stay with you.

Dear God, heal us with forgiveness.

Halfway House

Your light was on, and we hope to find a room for the night. This is as far as Mary can go. She will give birth tonight.

We leave our light on. People come and go here so the house number is important.

We also found your light. Mary needs a place to lie down. Can you help us?

She'll be safe here, but it's not the best place for a baby to be born.

We are ordinary people from a little town and do not need anything fancy.

I hope we won't offend you or the young mother with our lives and problems. We aren't angels.

The child was not sent to be born among angels. You live here?

Off and on. The people here come and go. Some stay for days, until they are sober or calmed down. Most were on cocaine or alcohol or both. They come here to get off drugs. That's who we are.

You seem to know each other. Like a family.

We have something in common. All of us have known the need for a high, a fix, a buzz.

The child was sent from on high.

That's another kind of high. We got our highs through our chemical of choice. Now we need to come down. Get straight.

Mary's high came to her in prayer, and she was visited by Gabriel from on high. Songs transport her.

As I said, this is no place for a young mother, or for a baby.

The child will grow to be a counselor, one who understands, listens. He will be a Mighty Counselor.

That's what we need, some mighty counseling. Someone who will listen, love, understand. Unconditionally. We might not be able to change; sometimes we just don't have the power.

The child will have the power for change. He is the power. He has come to share that power, to turn lives around.

Then you've come to the right place. We want that power. Wouldn't it be a miracle if the one thing we all want is what your baby will give us? A high from on High.

It will be a miracle. It is God's promise. We will join your family here. We will learn your names. The child will be born here for you.

Is that a promise?

It's a sure thing.

Dear God, come quickly and bring a miracle.

Nursing Home

WE NEED A ROOM, WE SAW THE LIGHT.
WILL YOU MAKE US A ROOM FOR JUST TONIGHT?

What a surprise! How can I help you?

We need a place for my wife, Mary. She will give birth tonight.

A birth here? This is a nursing home, and it is late. Our people are getting ready for sleep.

We will be quiet. She needs only a bed.

Right now all our staff is busy—giving out medicines and making sure no one falls while getting into their beds. Perhaps you could sit in the waiting room until someone is free to help you. The shift changes in an hour.

Mary's labor began awhile ago. Her contractions are closer and closer.

Why in the world did you come to a nursing home?

The light in the windows beckoned us. The people sitting in chairs so peacefully. The place looked like we'd be welcome.

These people are near the end of their years. Two are over one hundred years old.

They will like to have a child be born in their midst.

You might need a special nurse, a midwife.

Some of these old ones surely will remember how to help deliver, if we need them.

Most are grandparents, some are great-great grandparents. They love the little ones. Many are like little ones themselves.

This child will be their child. Mary will bear a child for them. For them to hold, to hold them.

Some will surely hold the child. Do you have a name chosen?

Jesus. We know it will be a boy, and his name will be called Jesus.

A good name. Our people know this name. The name is on their walls; they have memorized songs with this name. They have the name Jesus woven in their hearts.

Mary will tell them the story of the angel who visited her and surprised her beyond words. The angel who told her of the child to come, who gave her great promises about the child.

Was she frightened by the angel who visited?

First afraid. Then she believed.

That will be a good story for us to hear. Many here are afraid, then they believe. Some are only afraid as they grow older and closer to death.

Mary will tell them of her fear and faith. She knows a song to sing to all who fear. She will sing it softly, and it will bring them peace and joy.

Sing it here. It is growing quiet. Many will want to hear the song. There is room for you here in this place, room for you and the child.

Dear God, enter the hearts of the old and calm their fears.

Birthday Party

Welcome! This is a birthday party, as you can see. Some are leaving already, but you're not too late to join us.

We didn't know. We just noticed the balloons and streamers. Seemed so fitting for our own child—the one inside Mary, that is. This is Mary, I am Joseph. And I guess we're about ready for a birthday party.

Well, we're celebrating. We can celebrate as long as we want to; so come on in and join us.

It is nearly the due date of Mary's child. The child she carries. Mary needs a place to lie down. I suppose the party takes all your rooms?

At a party there is always room for something special—like guests, even guests who are expecting. Tell me about the child.

The birth was not something we planned. It was God's plan and God's gift.

That's often the case. When they come, you're sure glad; and you act like you wanted it all the time.

We did want a family. But we didn't know it would happen this way. We are both believers, and we've hoped for this child to come. Every Israelite mother had this hope since the time of Sarah.

Sarah and Abraham? The Old Testament couple? I've heard of them. That's a lot of years—from Abraham until now. What were you waiting for with all the others? Tell me what you mean.

We were waiting for the Messiah, the one who will bring joy to the world. God promised this child to kings and prophets and mothers for many generations. And Mary will give birth to the child that all believing mothers wished to bear. She is chosen of God.

Our birthday person will be honored to hear the story. If we had known you were coming, we might have made our preparations even more special—had a baby shower lined up.

The child's name will be Jesus. We have all we need for him: swaddling cloth, Mary's milk. God will provide.

Well, come. Join us. We are ready to light the candles on the cake.

Candles are important to any birth day. Generations will remember Jesus and his birth with candlelight. He will be a light in the world.

When we blow out the candles, you can make a wish for your child. It's our custom to make a wish for the birthday person, who also makes a wish.

We know what to wish for: that the child will make the lame to walk, the blind to see, the dead to rise. It is more than a wish; it is our hope, our belief.

What's the difference between wishing and hoping?

Hope has a promise to count on; our hope is that certain. God says, "Ask, and it will be given; knock and my door will be opened." We will tell you about our hope for the child after the candles are out.

Good. While we eat the cake, you can introduce yourselves. Everyone loves a baby. Then we'll all sing "Happy Birthday." Once for the birthday person, once for the child, Jesus.

Dear God, show us how to hope.

DECEMBER 11

House of Mourning

We saw all the people and hoped someone could give us shelter for one night. I am Joseph, this is Mary. She is with child and needs a place to give birth. I believe we have been sent here.

There has been a death in this home. These people have come to mourn, to weep. It is not a place for a birth.

The child will be born for this home. You may not understand now, but you will see that this child belongs in this place tonight.

An infant will cry. The family will hear the sound of a newborn. It is their child who died.

We have been taught this feeling, the mourning of Sarah and Abraham, of Rachel under her tree in Bethlehem. Death wakes an old cry in mothers and fathers.

Others here also have lost someone; they are here to offer comfort, to be together. There will be a time for new birth and hope. But first we must grieve.

Mary's child will be born for us all—also for this family, to release grieving and sorrow. He will know what you are feeling, that is why he has to be born.

How will a newborn infant know all this? It is hard even for the old who have learned well how to grieve.

The child will be named Jesus and Immanuel. A savior from sorrow and loss, a God who is with us. Jesus will be of God, of God's own Spirit. Jesus knows the heart of God, and of us.

We are all feeling and saying: God, why has this happened? Why did you not prevent this?

Tonight, the birth of Jesus will be a sign of life, of hope. His birth will be God speaking to you.

Their child's life ended. We waited so long for the birth. This death is what we are mourning.

Jesus' birth will show a life that never ends. A life that gives life to all— life that lasts forever.

You can see their child has died.

Their child is sleeping. There is a sleep we do not see, a breathing we do not hear. There is a life in a soul that lives.

That is what they want to believe, but first they will grieve.

Mary's child comes from where there is a Spirit who comforts.

Then stay. We will make room for a birth. We do not have all the answers. We are helpless. If your child's birth can make a difference, we will feel the blessing.

That is all we can do now, bless one another. Comfort. Be here. Be close to each other.

If they ask who you are will you introduce yourselves?

We will show the newborn child and tell who he is. Mary has a song she can whisper, when it is the right time. We will know.

Dear God, find us places to be silent and present.

Army Barracks

WE NEED A ROOM, WE SAW THE LIGHT.
WILL YOU MAKE US A ROOM FOR JUST TONIGHT?

I am Joseph, this is Mary who is with child.

How did you get into our place? Can I see your I.D.?

We are not known. The child inside her will make us known. The child holds our credentials.

A child who is not born holds your credentials? Is this some kind of joke?

It is a very joyful occasion, but it is no joke. The child to be born will be the Prince of Peace.

This is an army barracks. We don't have princes here; we have generals and captains and lieutenants. And corporals; I'm a corporal.

The child will cause lambs to lie down with lions. The child will be a Prince of Peace.

A real Prince of Peace would put our army out of business. Right now we are practicing peace. That's what we tell the men and women. We are training to keep peace in distant countries. This is big money. Do you know how many helicopters we just bought?

Mary is about to give birth. She needs a place in your barracks.

That is not possible. We have a good hospital, but right now our hospital is filled to capacity with patients.

Perhaps there is one bed, or a room where we can lay down a blanket.

She may hear some of the soldiers we just flew in. They are badly wounded. Some are delirious.

The child will be born to give peace on earth and good will to all humanity. There will be no more wounded soldiers. No more soldiers. No more war.

Tell our enemies. See all the places where we are fighting, sir.

The child's power comes from the spirit of God. Mary is filled with God's spirit; that is how she is pregnant.

Sounds like something out of Ripley's Believe It Or Not.

That's right, some will believe it and some will not believe.

I'll call a jeep and we'll drive you to the hospital. You sure she won't mind the crying and the shouting? There's a lot of pain and suffering in that hospital. A lot of stuff inside those wounded soldiers that needs to get healed.

The child is coming to heal pain and suffering and what is inside us all. Peace is something he will bring to the heart.

By the time he grows up, I'll be retired and get Social Security. And if what you say is true, there won't be a job for me much longer.

There will always be soldiers.

I thought you said he'd be Prince of Peace, in all the world.

It will only work when he comes into people's hearts. Some will not let him in.

Figured there was a catch to all this. Well, let's get you and Mary over to that hospital now. And then we'll see what that baby can do.

Dear God, come into our hearts with peace.

Food Shelter

Just who is knocking on the door?

The two of us, and the baby in her. She will give birth.

We are already too many. I have two at my breast and one inside me. There is no room, no food here. We are starving.

The one to be born of Mary is the Son of God.

What can he do for these two trying to find milk?

He will save people from their sin.

I am not thinking of sin; I'm worried about food. We need bread and rice and milk.

The sin is indifference, lack of love. The child will take away the indifference and lack of love that keep others from sharing. And then there will be more than enough food for mothers and fathers like you.

But he is still inside his mother. It will be too late to help me and these children. My two will starve before he grows; only one will live.

We will name Mary's child Jesus. He will take care of the child who will live. He will heal and teach mothers and fathers how to live, how to care.

And there will be no more hunger?

There will be hunger. But there will also be compassion and courage and a plentiful harvest that waits to be shared.

There are other children and mothers and fathers here, too.

In this room?

You are at the door of a world of children starving and thirsting.

Is there room among you for Mary to give birth to the child?

If you want to give birth in a world of hunger and poverty, you are at the right place.

The child is coming. He will bring food to the hungry and compassion to the coldhearted.

Then let the one who will save us be born here.

Mary's child is the one who will save you. Where is the bed where she will give birth?

Where I birthed all ten. In our bed, this blanket, this blanket on the ground.

Where are the others?

Where these will go, unless someone will save them soon.

Dear God, change our hearts and divide the food.

Five-Star Hotel

WE NEED A ROOM, WE SAW THE LIGHT.
WILL YOU MAKE US A ROOM FOR JUST TONIGHT?

I am Joseph from Nazareth, and this is my wife, Mary. We just arrived; it was a long journey. As you can see, Mary is pregnant.

Do you have a reservation?

No. We took the chance that you might give us a room.

Would you like a suite on the sixteenth floor? The view is facing east. Tomorrow you can see the sun rise if you are up.

Mary will be too occupied to watch the sun rise.

There is a sauna, hot tub, and kitchenette. It's a perfect place for a honeymoon couple. Who recommended our hotel to you?

This is the first hotel we came to.

You know we're a five-star hotel. That speaks for itself.

The only star I know of is the star of David. That is why we made the trip, to be registered as Jews.

So, you're both Jewish. This is a chain hotel; we are in thirteen countries—also in Israel.

We need only one bed. Now she needs a simple place to lie down.

Nothing is simple here. The cheapest room we have goes for two hundred and seventy dollars for two. Perhaps that is what you want.

We are poor people. We thought you might have a bed, just a bed. I can lay down my cloak for her to lie on. We are used to sleeping on ground.

Street people don't stay in our place. We are glad to take a credit card. We lock doors in thirty minutes and only guests with key cards can enter.

We are peasant people, but the child in her is royal. The world will hear of his fame: King of Kings, Prince of Peace. The world will know of your generosity.

We like free publicity. Are you sure he will make us known?

I am sure. He is of the lineage of Abraham and the household of King David.

Hmmm. Perhaps for this I will make an exception. I'll give Mary and you one night free in exchange for the publicity. I'll just record that you're with a travel agency.

What you do for this child will be made known in all the world.

Let a bellhop show you the room. We will put you on the top floor.

The child will be known as the highest.

If you have anything to give the bellhop he will be grateful.

I will ask Mary. She has a song.

Remember: in the morning the news reporters will come.

Mary can sing for them, too.

Dear God, bless us with your presence and your song.

Boarding House

You look weary. Come in. How can we help?

We are looking for a night's lodging. Every hotel is filled. Mary here is with child. We expect the birth tonight.

I don't know if a child was ever born in these rooms. I've lived here since not long after the place was built, and it never happened during my time. I could rent a room for one night. But if you are going to have a child . . .

The child to be born is not our child. He was given to Mary by God, and his birth will be greeted with joy by people everywhere, of all times.

You mean, the birth can be memorialized—maybe with a plaque over the door? We've never had anything that special happen here.

I mean the kind of memorial handed down from generation to generation— people telling other people, keeping the story alive forever.

I think we have the kind of people here who will do that. We all know what's going on around here. You can't really have many secrets.

It is a birth to talk about for years to come, to tell to the whole world.

Some of the people who live here are older; they travel a lot, and their stories go with them. They'd tell the story if it truly is a good one.

It is a story they'll make their own, as though the infant is their own.

Most don't have children living here; some don't have children at all. We also have young singles who travel a lot in their work. We're a pretty close group here, like family. I'm sure they could get into it, if it happened in this place.

Mary knows the child is not just her own; he will belong to all the people in the house. He will belong to us all. That is the wonder of this one in Mary.

Do you intend to stay for a while?

We will stay only for the birth. It is in his birth that the child will belong to you and those in this house, in his birth and in his life and in his death. But we will not stay here long.

Where do you intend to go next?

The child will go into the whole world. We will follow him to the end. We were told a child will lead us. We believe this and we are prepared to follow him.

He will need a lot of help; a newborn can't do very much on his own.

Inside him is God's plan and purpose. When we hear him, we will hear God. We will watch him grow in wisdom and stature, and in favor with God.

We all like growing in wisdom; you can't be too smart nowadays.

He will show God's wisdom. His life will unfold God's will. When you are all together, we can tell the rest of the story. We've only told you the beginning. Mary will do it in a song.

Dear God, unfold your will to us.

Family Meal

WE NEED A ROOM, WE SAW THE LIGHT.
WILL YOU MAKE US A ROOM FOR JUST TONIGHT?

What a surprise. We are starting to eat our dinner. What can I do for you?

I am Joseph, Mary is with me, and she is with child.

It's not a big house. We have four children and there's a bedroom for each. That's how we planned it. No guest room, really.

We only need a place for the birth, and then we will go on.

Shhh. Not too loud. The children will hear, and you know how kids are. They'll want you to stay. I have a long day ahead tomorrow, and was planning to get up early. A birth isn't what I had in mind.

Mary will try to keep the child still. Except for the birth cry. Then she will nurse him. His name is Jesus. We have already named him.

A popular name. We all know the name. Don't know anyone who uses it much anymore, though—as a name that is.

We did not choose the name; Gabriel the archangel gave Mary the name. It came from God.

You're lucky to get a name that way. We went through hundreds of names to choose ours. We had to buy books.

Jesus can be born in your home this night.

It would seem special to have a baby named Jesus born in this house. Our children were all born in St. Joseph's Hospital.

That is my name: Joseph. Do you hear Mary's breathing? She may be in early labor.

I will ask the family. Please wait in the vestibule. I'll keep the door open until we decide. [Pause]

What did you decide?

We didn't have time to discuss it. I said: "A couple needs a place to give birth—to a baby named Jesus. They want to stay here, to give birth in our house. But there's no room."

We are sorry.

No, wait. Then the children each said, "Give them my room." Now we have four rooms for Mary and her child. Our children are deciding which room to pick.

We are grateful. Your house will never be the same. This child will be a member of your family. [Pause]

Just before you came, we gave thanks with the prayer, "Come Lord Jesus, be our guest." Our little one asked what that meant. The children have decided: yours will be the room of the little one who asked, "What does it mean?"

What is the little one's name?

We named her Anna, after her grandmother.

Anna is the name of Jesus' grandmother, Mary's mother.

In the morning the children will have a song for the baby.

Dear God, make thanks our prayer, make our heart your room.

Prison

WE NEED A ROOM, WE SAW THE LIGHT.
WILL YOU MAKE US A ROOM FOR JUST TONIGHT?

Who is that at the gate?

Mary from Nazareth, who is with child—and I, Joseph, her husband.

Why do you come here?

Mary will soon give birth. We need a room.

Who sent you to this place?

We found it in the night. The lights in the towers showed us the way.

This is a maximum-security prison. The lights are on so we can see if any prisoners try to escape.

We need only a spare room for her and the child. I can wait in the hallway or lobby.

There is no spare room or hallway or lobby. Every room is a cell with a lock and bolt.

A cell will be all right. She needs only a place to lie down.

It's just a tiny, hard bed, a board and a thin mattress.

Would you have such a cell for her and the child?

We have one cell left. But it is in the center of the prison. It can get noisy when the prisoners are restless. And they are often restless at this time of year.

Perhaps the child's birth will calm them, keep them company.

They don't need company. Each has a private cell. We enforce solitary confinement here. And what about the noise?

Mary will not be bothered by the noise. She waits for the cry of the child.

How long will you stay after the child comes?

We will leave whenever you need the room. The child needs only to be born here. Then we can leave.

The child needs to be born here? In a maximum-security prison?

Yes. Here.

Who is this woman? Who is the child?

The woman is Mary. Her child will be named Jesus. Savior. He will save people from fear, from darkness, from sin, from prison.

These prisoners are here for life. They cannot escape.

The child will set them free inside. The child will set their minds free, their hearts.

That would be a miracle, that would.

This child is God's miracle.

That's what we need in this place: miracles. Come, then. I'll show you to the cell.

Dear God, give us a quiet miracle that frees us.

Day Care Center

Hello. Do you wish to enroll a child?

Our child is still in his mother; he will be born soon.

The waiting list is long. We don't start here until their third birthday.

We were not thinking of enrolling the child. We need a room for his birth.

That's never been done here before. A birth in a day care center! That would be something special.

This birth is indeed special, but we did not make it that way. The child to be born is the Son of God. And Mary needs a room soon.

You mean Jesus? Oh my! But a room? That will be very hard to find in our center.

It can be a room where there are no children, the office, the kitchen, a storage room. A rug or coat will do for a bed. We are used to sleeping on the ground.

Oh, I'm sure we can find something better than that. A place where the children can come and see the mother and the baby. This can make a great show-and-tell.

Mary has a lot she can tell the children. A story of angels and of the Holy Spirit of God—a story of visions and dreams.

Children like fairy tales; they like drawing pictures of angels.

Mary's stories are truth; they need only to be heard and then believed.

The children will believe. That's what children do well—especially stories about a baby inside a mother.

Then Mary can sing her song about the baby.

What a wonderful program, such a surprise! Jesus born here.

It is a surprise, though the birth was predicted by many through the years.

The children will want to touch the baby inside the mother. They can lay their fingers against her and feel the baby move. Can we do that before the birth?

The children can be among the first to touch and know, and believe.

The children will want to ask Mary about her mother and family, and about you. And, most of all, about the baby.

His name, "Jesus," means savior. An angel of the Lord named him Jesus, for he will save the children of the world.

The children will love to hear that story. Will you tell the children what you have just said, and about the meaning of his name?

I will tell them. When you have shown us the room, we will wait for the children. Mary will sing a song, and we will tell the story of the child.

And the children can draw angels with finger paints. We will hang them in the room, to decorate the place, and make it as beautiful as the story you have told me.

We will look for the children to come, to be excited.

It's all so beautiful; just like a story we tell the children every year. It's as though the story became real in our very own place.

Dear God, make us into children.

House of Loss

WE NEED A ROOM, WE SAW THE LIGHT.
WILL YOU MAKE US A ROOM FOR JUST TONIGHT?

I am Joseph. Mary needs a room to bear her child. We saw the candle in the window. Perhaps the birth can add to your holiday celebration.

We always have this candle burning during holidays. It keeps alive a memory. This is a hard time for us. The loss of our baby raises a yearning in us. The candle reminds us; the candle does not feel like a celebration.

The child who is to be born will have a short life on earth. When he leaves us here, he will show us more that is to come.

They go away too soon. Even if they are grown, it seems too fast. There's no stopping hurt and death.

Mary knows this already. Loss is in her song. She will need your candle tonight, for the life and the death of this child.

We have shared the candle with many. Others who have lost children have been here, and we have reminisced. Sometimes nostalgia comes as a heavy wave over us. We have cried often beside this candle.

Mary knows the feeling in her heart. She says pain pierces her like a sharp sword.

We know the feeling. We grieve this time every year. It is our time of loss.

Prophets predicted that this child will suffer and die. God gives each of us a lifetime; for some it is long, for some it is not.

We have a room we prepared for our beloved baby—a room we never used. Some things are still in the room. The room is to us a holy space. Sometimes we need to go there for a while; sometimes we try not to go there. We are torn.

This is the right room for Mary and her child. A place where we can waken to the feelings you have mentioned. In the birth, we also will share with you this loss of losing a child, of being torn. All birth moves toward loss.

We will light one more candle in the room, to cast enough light for the birth. [Sigh] The candle gets lit, the candle goes out.

But not the fire that lights the candle. The child will have many names; Light is one of the names. He comes to bring light that shines through loss, beyond death. Light and life that never end.

That is what we want most of all. The other side of what seems like the end. The light on the other side.

This child of light will lead us through the end. And on the other side, there is only life and light and love. Life is at the other end.

We will shut the door to this room. Sometimes there is a draft through this part of the house. It could snuff out the candle.

A fire will burn all night. You will see light in the morning.

Dear God, send the light that puts out darkness.

Wedding Reception

Hello, can we help you? We're in the middle of a wedding party.

We saw all the people and knew there would be someone if we needed help.

This party is by invitation only. I don't think we know you.

I'm Joseph of Nazareth. This is Mary. As you can see she is near labor.

This is really embarrassing. I know how difficult it is to be pregnant, but they're cutting the cake, and in a little while we're going to dance.

We didn't come to be guests or to dance, only to find a place to birth the child.

That would be a first in our town, a birth at a wedding.

This child is the Son of God, a first for us all.

The Son of God! Well, I am glad you feel the child is special. Too many just have babies and don't give the kid's future a thought.

There are great plans for his future. He will be known in every land. Through this child all of us will be blessed.

I had hopes like that for one of our children but it didn't turn out that way. But maybe you could bring good luck to this wedding. The bride and groom are people we love; they will need all the blessings they can get.

Mary's child can help.

But where can we put you? All these people have the run of the house. There isn't a room for privacy. How can a baby be born while we're celebrating and dancing?

Mary and I will enjoy the music and the laughter. We are glad for this birth. We will let the joy welcome the child to earth. We were all born while someone was being glad, and in the dancing mood.

My parents still talk about how glad they were the night I was born.

It should be that way for all. Mary is looking for a joyful place to deliver.

I wonder what it would be like for us to show the baby to all the wedding party? Oh, look: it's time for the toast. Step into the hallway with me. We will find a room for you when the toast has been made.

I have a toast I can offer them. And we have a song of joy and gladness. Mary can sing it well; you will not be ashamed. It is a song about their future.

This wedding is about the future. Come in then, and let me introduce you.

Dear God, be with us in what's ahead.

Bible Study

Have you room for the three of us?

I see only you and the woman.

I am Joseph. Mary's baby is coming, as you can see. Then there will be three.

That's very interesting. That's the subject we're studying tonight in my house: "He is coming." It's a Bible study.

So you are expecting us.

No, no, not at all. Not in this way. We are reading together, studying the prophets, about Jesus coming into the world. We didn't think. . . . I mean, no one would believe it could happen in modern times.

The child in her is Jesus. He needs to be born in your home.

We know about Jesus.

This child will save you from sin, death, and the power of the devil.

I know that sentence from a catechism lesson. Is this some kind of program you two are putting on?

We are here for the birth of Jesus. He needs a place to come into the world. Please. We need a shelter, a room.

You must think we're in some kind of a Christmas drama. The child's home is supposed to be Bethlehem. Right? Well, this is the United States, and I wasn't informed of being part of a play tonight. We are reading Isaiah—just finished the promise that Jesus would be "Prince of Peace." We're talking about that right now.

He is the Prince of Peace inside you—inside everyone. It means the child will give you rest. He can be born in this place tonight. Inside you, too.

We're not into being born again. Sounds like our neighbors. You might be more comfortable spending the night with them.

We were led to your house tonight. And Mary has a song you will all like.

Our program is very full, we've got a lot to cover. But maybe she can sing for our closing. I hope it's a religious song. We close that way.

The song is called Magnificat. The song is about her child.

We all know that song; we read it right here—the Gospel of Luke. It fits in with our study of the prophets.

The Magnificat is about tonight, about peace, about God's grace in this place.

We usually have refreshments after the study. You introduce yourselves then, and then Mary can sing. Then the others will leave.

Mary can give birth to the child here?

We'll see. There are three empty bedrooms. Our children are in college. One is in the seminary.

Dear God, what are we to learn?

Tavern

WE NEED A ROOM, WE SAW THE LIGHT.
WILL YOU MAKE US A ROOM FOR JUST TONIGHT?

Who is knocking on our door?

Joseph, a carpenter, and Mary, who is with child.

Are you married?

We are betrothed. I have promised to be her husband.

But she is pregnant, you say. She is with child.

She is with child. The child is near due now. The child is not mine, it is a child of God's Holy Spirit.

Hmmm. You mean she's pregnant by another man?

The child in her is Immanuel, the Son of God.

Do you really expect me to believe that?

No. But we hope you will believe it, pray you will believe it.

Right. And now you are looking for a place to give birth.

That is why we are here.

This is a neighborhood bar. People come here to drink, to have a good time.

We need only a little place, for a little while.

If I let you in, it'll be straight to the back room. Don't start talking to my customers about this girl being pregnant by God. When they see you, they will ask about you.

Tell them what you will.

What is your nationality?

We are Jewish. We go back to Father Abraham, to Sarah. We come from Nazareth.

I can't tell you're Jewish. My customers won't be able to notice unless you say something. Not one of my customers is Jewish. We're all from the same part of the world. So best to keep quiet.

We only want a place for the birth of the child.

What will you name the child?

Jesus. That is the name he was given by God's angel.

Jesus. Jesus. We use that name a lot around here.

This is the Jesus who will save the people—people who call his name. When the child is born, we will bring him out to show them the child whose name they are calling. They will know when they look at Jesus.

Hey, what is the mother singing?

She is singing about what people in this room want: hope.

Well, then, come ahead; take the back room. Let's have the sound of a new life in this old place. And when the child is born, bring him out to show us, like you said. We need something to lift out spirits.

Dear God, birth us new life.

Bus Depot

Step up to the ticket counter. How many are you?

Three of us. The child who is still inside Mary makes three.

You don't have to pay for an unborn child. Where are you going?

Here. We just arrived.

Then you won't need a ticket. You won't need to stand in line. This is only for people who are going somewhere.

We are going somewhere: into all the world. That's the information we have. The child in Mary will go into all the world.

We don't have bus routes into all the world. This is domestic travel and we only have limited bus connections.

We're not going into all the world now, only when the child comes.

Well, what can I do for you now?

We need a loving place for Mary to give birth. We see you have a nativity scene by the tree in the corner. So we knew you'd understand.

I know what the Nativity and the creche is all about. We put that stuff up every year. But I don't understand this business of helping a mother with a place to give birth—in a bus depot. There must be better options. We have rules.

We did not intend for the child to be born here. But we just arrived from our home in Galilee, and the child is stirring in his mother.

The only place I can think of is behind me, where all the baggage is stored. I hate to think a kid would have to be born between suitcases and boxes.

The child will live with the humble, the lepers, the outcasts.

We don't have leprosy in our country. Dirt we've got, and AIDS and drugs and cancer and outcasts.

Jesus, the child, will live with thieves and robbers and prostitutes and addicts and people who are sick and dying. He will save thieves and robbers and those addicted or afflicted or dying.

Save them? Well, we have plenty of those around. I wouldn't want his job. That's asking a lot of a kid who isn't born yet.

Mary has high hopes for her child. These things were promised to her.

My wife had a similar notion before our kids were born. She hoped they'd grow up to be social workers and go into the Peace Corps. One of them thinks she's making a difference.

She is making a difference, and Jesus will make a difference. Mary is ready for the room. People behind us waiting for their tickets. Can you show us the place?

Follow me. You say her name is Mary, and the baby's name is Jesus. Your name?

Joseph. We have been chosen to care for this child. The songs that are playing near the crèche are songs about Mary's child.

We sure like them. Makes this bus depot a lot friendlier, peaceful.

Love and peace. That is why the child has come.

Dear God, love is a place to be.

Department Store

WE NEED A ROOM, WE SAW THE LIGHT.
WILL YOU MAKE US A ROOM FOR JUST TONIGHT?

We saw the Christmas display in your store window and hoped you could help us find a room for this night. I am Joseph, and Mary is ready to give birth. She feels the baby coming.

Hey, Joseph and Mary? Really? And Mary is about to have her baby? Wow! Well, this is a department store, not a hotel. But it's a great time for you to come by. We're in the middle of a big holiday promotion.

We only want a room. We're not wanting to make money because of the birth. The child in her, Jesus, is our wealth and our riches.

You'll get some of the profit, don't worry. And we'll find you a room. It's worth it for us. What would help most is if Mary could hold off the birth for at least an hour or two so we can get a camera crew in. This will look great on the morning news. What a scoop for our store that you chose this place for the birth.

We did not choose. There was no other place open. Yours is the last light we saw in town. Mary is in labor.

Please hang on. We can set up the cameras soon; they're stored just down the street. Our company president will phone them to hurry.

Mary is weary. We have been traveling for a long time. The child is the Son of God: Jesus.

What a break for our company. Especially with the economic slump. We'll get close-ups of you and Mary. People like seeing the eyes and expressions. She has a look that will really sell. And the baby—we'll cover the news with pictures of the baby. We'll roll these films every year. If you want we'll make out a contract so the baby can get royalties in the future. Think of the money.

This birth is not about money and royalties. This is about the heart. The child will bring peace and joy, he is not here to bring money.

Peace and joy. I could do with those. Peace especially. Sometimes I feel like finding another job, another way of living—especially at this time of year. I'm in overload most of the time.

The child will help with those burdens; he will make a heavy day be light.

That's what I'm talking about. It's after hours and here I am planning for a big advertising shoot. It's too much. Except for the sales, laughing all the way to the bank. But these days I don't do much of that; I'm losing my laughter.

The child will bring joy to the whole world—to you, too. But now Mary needs a room for the birth. The story will get out, even without cameras and film. The angel of God made this promise. You will hear all about it.

Okay. All right. We'll give you the studio for the birth. We'll shut down the lights and get out of here and give you peace.

Thank you. Mary has a song that can calm you, help ease those burdens. It is called Magnificat.

Well, make yourself at home. She can sing while I pack my brief-case, check my voice mail, and send a couple of e-mails.

Dear God, turn exploitation into good will.

Intensive Care Unit

WE NEED A ROOM, WE SAW THE LIGHT.
WILL YOU MAKE US A ROOM FOR JUST TONIGHT?

Hello. Are we at the right door? Are there beds here?

Wait. Someone will come to help you.

My wife is in labor; we need a bed.

She should be down one floor—in the maternity area. This is intensive care.

She asked to come here for the birth.

This unit is for patients who need special attention.

We saw that on the sign, but Mary wants intensive care for the child. This is no ordinary birth.

All mothers feel that way, that their child is special.

Mary is sure of it. Gabriel told her.

Dr. Gabriel? I don't know who that might be, but we cannot make an exception. Sorry. No babies born here.

She is sure this is where she is to deliver—in this place of intensive care. The child's name will be Jesus; he will save the lives of people.

That's what this unit is all about—saving lives that might easily be lost.

Mary wants her child to be born in such a place. Saving life is what he will do for a living.

The child will be a nurse? A doctor?

He will be a healer. He will make people well, make blind people see, make lame people walk.

Shhh. Keep your voice down. Some of the people here are critically ill, some are near death.

This child will raise the dead to life again.

Raise the dead to life? You mustn't raise such hopes here. Perhaps I should call the hospital chaplain to talk with you. But this is the lunch hour and I cannot leave; we are short-staffed.

The child will be born soon. Please . . .

All right. Come into this cubicle. Let her lie down here. I will draw the curtain and call the birthing unit to tell them we are making this exception.

Thank you. You will see that Mary's child is an exception. He is the Son of God. His birth will bring life and healing to this place, and to the whole world.

Here, take this warm blanket. It will keep Mary warm.

Thank you. You will be blessed for taking us in.

Dear God, save us in our emergencies and give us Christmas life.

DECEMBER 26
House of Anger

WE NEED A ROOM, WE SAW THE LIGHT.

WILL YOU MAKE US A ROOM FOR JUST TONIGHT?

We heard the loud sounds and were sure someone was still up. We need lodging: the newborn child is Jesus. Mary is his mother, I am Joseph.

Sometimes our voices go right through the walls. Our feelings yell. We are angry, bitter. Sorry if you heard us.

Your voices led us to this place. The child already knows about anger and bitterness. Even inside his mother, he felt the anger of the streets, between armies, the bitterness of the poor. He was born for the sake of anger, for the sake of bitterness.

When I was born, I cried. We all begin with crying.

The child will save us from bitter weeping. Who in the world does not want to be saved from anger? He will cry with you.

You could find a friendlier place to stay. Next door, they seem peaceful. Never raising their voices, that we've heard.

The child has come to heal. This home is where we will stay.

Sometimes we don't talk for days. Feelings churn deep inside. We feel tense in our sleep and when we wake. In our home, tension can last for days. More. And then it explodes. It was this way before us. Part of our genes.

The child is conceived by God's own Spirit: he has a royal lineage, a holy family.

Why would you bring a royal child, a newborn, into a house ready to explode?

The child is learning that all places have anger. It is an angry world. He will learn to live in a hostile world, to heal the anger.

Our anger cuts us off from each other. We walk away, look down, slam a door, don't listen. We demand the last word—an angry word.

This child will know about prisons, barriers, shouting, having the last word. He will be called the first Word. That Word that creates, heals.

Healing words. We don't hear those here.

You will hear them, even from this infant. He will give you words of peace. This child will do miracles with words, turn anger into affection; he will turn hate into love.

Then this is where he must stay, this house of anger. Tomorrow we will invite our friends and families, for they know of our anger. We are not alone in this.

He will weep for this house, for your city, for your nation. His tears will heal.

When I am angry I see fire, a red-hot fire.

The child will help you see light, candlelight.

Then please stay. Choose any room you want. We have been angry in all of them. The child can stay forever, if he can stand whatever happens. If he can heal. If he needs to learn more, I know many other homes like this.

Dear God, break our burdens, heal our anger.

Airport

WE NEED A ROOM, WE SAW THE LIGHT.

WILL YOU MAKE US A ROOM FOR JUST TONIGHT?

Mary, the line is very long. Here there are no soldiers guarding, keeping the line going, shouting. The wait may be long, so we'll take turns holding the child. I can't tell if the flight is on time.

I couldn't help overhearing. Many flights have been cancelled. When we get to the desk, this flight might be wiped off the board.

The crowd is murmuring. They look worried.

I'd give you my place, but I've been standing here for two hours. It's upsetting to be running late; makes the trip quite unpleasant. Where are you going?

We'll take whatever flight is going tonight, to anywhere in the world. Our child is a citizen of the Earth.

You have your passports?

We'll tell them about the child at the ticket counter. We'll say his name. We'll explain the promises, the hopes. Mary knows all the information by heart. She knows more than is on a passport. Oh look, the line has stopped.

They have cancelled the flight. We'll have to go to another counter. When we know which one, we'll hurry to get nearer the front of the next line.

Mary and I will bring Jesus when we know where to go.

Follow me. I'll take you there when they. . . . Wait. I see it now— the one with the green light. I will hurry and hold you a place.

We can wait. We're not in as great a hurry as many of these people. They look so tired; some are angry, worried, disappointed. They will not get to their destination on time.

This flight is scheduled for Rome. Is that your final destination?

We have not been there. In Rome they will find a place for Mary and the child to rest. And if this plane is filled we can take another flight.

The other goes to Cairo, Egypt.

Egypt. That is a place we have heard of, though we have not been there. The child will learn these places by heart: Rome, Egypt. Where do you live?

San Francisco. Have you been there?

We have not. We come from Bethlehem. But the child Jesus will someday go there, I'm sure. Gabriel promised the child would be born for all people. You go to the new counter. We may see you there.

I will save you a place. Try to hurry. No need to run, but hurry.

The child does not like to hurry. There seems to be a timepiece inside the child that knows when we're going too fast. Perhaps we'll see you at the gate.

But you have no passport for going to another country? I wish you could go with me. I want to see what they say about the passport.

The angel said the child will go to all people. That is what we believe. Mary knows what to say. The child will be allowed to go, and we will go with him.

You can have my seat if they're overbooked.

We'll find a place, even if we don't sit together. Mary will hold the child.

I would take a turn to hold the child, if he will let me.

Dear God, let us hold the Child as we journey.

Family Devotions

Hello. I am Joseph, and this is my wife, Mary, and our newborn child, Jesus. This doesn't seem a good time for you. Everything is so very quiet.

We're in the middle of devotions. Praying. We do it at the table every night. I learned the habit when I was little. I want our children to do the same.

May we join in your prayer? Prayer is how we got here. They have shut their eyes. Let them pray; we will stand nearby to listen and to pray with them.

They are praying about being more open, more concerned about ones with greater needs. The news tonight was very hard to see: floods, earthquakes, refugees, those with no shelter.

We know. We saw the poor on our journey, the homeless, the hurting. The ones outside the city limits cried for help. We had too little to give.

There's always something to give. We are praying about the wealth we have in our own family, about sharing with others. We voted tonight in our family to buy a goat for a family we will never see.

You did this in the name of your whole family? A good gift.

We are doing it in the name of Jesus. That is the name we are using. Inside the card, where we write our greeting and name, we are adding: This goat is given in Jesus' name.

Mary and I know how great the gift of food can be. There is a gift Mary and I need now.

Our family is wide open to giving. Today we lost a dear friend to death. We are wide open to filling the gap.

We can be your new friends. We need a place to stay.

She came each week to clean, and to cook for the children when we were on the road. She served us, served our needs. We called her Sister; she was family.

Tonight we can take her place. The child will do for others what Sister did.

Sister told us sad and beautiful stories about her great-great grandmother, who was born in a slave hut and escaped to freedom on the underground railroad. The stories help to make us care, make us love our freedom.

The child will set slaves free, make slaves into priests and rulers. He will establish a kingdom on earth called Justice. The child is named Jesus.

Sister would like knowing her place is being filled by someone named Jesus. She often spoke the name Jesus in her prayers. She said his name as though he lived here, walking right beside her. And she was sure he'd meet her at Grand Central Station.

You mean heaven.

That's what she called it, Grand Central Station. That's where she got off the train and was a free woman—even freer than her great-great grandmother.

Dear God, bring justice and freedom.

Home Communion

WE NEED A ROOM, WE SAW THE LIGHT.
WILL YOU MAKE US A ROOM FOR JUST TONIGHT?

Thank you for opening the door. I didn't know you were homebound. You are in a walker; I'm sorry for the trouble.

Oh, no problem. I have been in this walker for seven years. My minister is here and we're getting ready for Holy Communion.

Mary and I are weary from a long journey. She needs a place to nurse the child. We are sorry for the bother.

You are welcome here. I can show you to a room, but my pastor has everything set out for the Lord's Supper. It won't take long, if you can wait. The Lord's Supper is important to me.

We are Jewish and belong to a synagogue in Nazareth. We would be happy to wait.

There's a synagogue on High Street, ten minutes from here.

We aren't looking for a synagogue; Mary needs only a quiet place to lie down and to nurse the baby. The child's name is Jesus.

That is very interesting. We believe in a Jesus who came to earth many years ago and is coming again. In this meal we ask him to come once more to us, in us.

The child whom Mary holds has been coming for many years. He is the one we believed was coming in our meal of Seder. We ate the parsley dipped in salt water and felt him coming, to bring joy into our sorrow and tears.

We have those feelings in this meal: sorrow and joy. We believe he joins us in both of these, that he gives us life, even in our death. Joy, even in our sorrow.

The angel promised Mary that God's Son would be inside her, fill her miraculously, and she would give birth to Jesus.

The minister will say to me, "Take and eat, this is the body of Christ." Each time I take Communion, I imagine being filled with Jesus in some way. When I believe I am filled with a new spirit, a clean spirit, God's Holy Spirit.

In the Seder, we eat unleavened bread and drink wine. The bread we eat is called Aphikoman, which means, "He is coming."

That is what I like about when the minister comes; that in the meal he brings, Christ comes to me, to us, into me. And I will come to Christ, both ways.

Many will call this child Christ, the Messiah, the anointed one. But now, he is a hungry child. You can hear his cries. Could you show us to that room so Mary can nurse him?

Of course, of course. I know the feeling, and the sound. Come to my living room, and Mary can nurse him on my old sofa. It's been in the family for sixty years. I once gave birth to a daughter there.

We thank you. The child thanks you. We are grateful for your kindness.

I will introduce my minister to you later. I am sure he will be glad to meet you.

Thank you for your good spirit.

❦

Dear God, give us a spirit that blesses.

Refugee Camp

Hey, where do you think you're going? You don't want to enter this camp. The child is so young. Do not expose your infant to our illnesses.

We have come to be with you for a night. Then we will move on.

You *want* to be here tonight? I can see you're strangers in this area. Are you with a medical team? Disaster relief? Where are they staying overnight?

We are on our own.

Typhoid has broken out in our camp. First the earthquake and flood, now this. This is no place for a child.

The mother and I agreed to come here.

Agreed to come? Who sent you?

The Spirit of God. We are not in charge of this journey. This child born of Mary is not her own.

That's a strange way to look at your child. Whose is he?

The child's name is Jesus. He belongs to the Lord and to the world. And so we are visiting the world. We are beginning our visit in this place.

Trying to expose the child to typhoid so you can immunize him?

Exposed, perhaps, but not to typhoid. Getting the child used to what is to be done in his life, to be with the sick and hurting.

It could kill him, you know that.

We know that it could. But we also know that Jesus will grow to live, to live fully, then he will die. And not of a disease like typhoid.

How do you know what will kill the child?

His fate was chosen before his birth. The child will not die because he visits and cares for those who are sick; he will be put to death by those who do not love.

So you are spending the night to teach your child how to love?

The child has many names. One of his names is Love. It was really the child who brought us here.

Well, that is certainly what we need, love in all kinds of ways: medicine, food, drink, to be held and comforted.

Mary knows a song of comfort. If she sings here at the gate, perhaps others will come from outside to visit, to love, to help, and even to live here with you.

She's welcome to sing. We need people who will love us in our sickness and our fear. It's just that I worry about the child. We'll find a place for Mary to sing near the gate.

After the song we will walk through your camp, to all the beds, so the child can see everyone.

Be sure they see the child. Hold up the child so they can see his face. Please tell them the things you've told me. About love and hope and caring and life.

Dear God, make love our best medicine.

New Year's Watch

WE NEED A ROOM, WE SAW THE LIGHT.

WILL YOU MAKE US A ROOM FOR JUST TONIGHT?

We followed the ringing of the bell, and knew something special was happening. So we brought the child.

We always ring out the old year with the church bell. That's how we say goodbye. We've done it as long as I can remember. Ringing bells is my thing.

You're all alone. Where are all the others?

Everyone waits for it to happen. Wherever they are, they know this bell is closing the old year.

We want the baby to hear the bells, it's a sound he can remember.

I began doing this when I was little. All I had to do is walk up the hill at 11:30 and ring the bell for twenty-five minutes. We'd wait five, and at midnight ring in the new year. Still do it that way.

Ringing in a new time.

A new year of our Lord. I always felt God was really close just before midnight. That was the best part, but also a hard time— those last minutes of the old year.

Letting go is hard to do. Letting go of the past. Already his mother is letting go. She knows something old will pass, and something new will begin.

In those five minutes between years, some turn on their lights. They flick them as a sign that something very special is happening.

This is a good place for us to be tonight. The church, the bells. I am Joseph, and this is Mary. Mary's child is the beginning of a new time.

I always felt each baby gets a chance to do something new.

You are stopping the bells now. Is this the time?

I try to be exact with the time of midnight. It seems that in this little time the past and the future meet.

The prophets call it the fullness of time—where past and future meet. It is the time when this child was born. He came in God's fullness of time.

It happens each year at this time. Life gets born all over again.

Look: the baby is waking. He will hear the bell begin the new year.

Go outside and watch the yard lights flicker, see your breath, see the stars in the dark skies. Listen to the sound of the ringing.

Mary's child knows about stars. He knows about night and day, birds of the air and fish of the sea. We will look for a star in the east.

I know a song, "Star of the East, O Bethlehem Star."

We don't know the song but we know the star.

Later I will sing the song to you and Mary and to the child. In the new year.

Then Mary will sing the "Magnificat." It tells what happens in the fullness of time, the time you just showed us—between the old and the new.

Look, the child is smiling. What is his name? What do you call him?

His name is Jesus. He is called Savior, Mighty God, Prince of Peace.

Dear God, move us from old to new.

New Year's Party

Look, Mary: people are coming and coming, no one is leaving. The place is full, and still they come. I like the music; the baby will like it, too.

Hello, and welcome. We always have a party this time of year. People whom we haven't seen for years have come. Many don't even have an invitation.

I am Joseph. This is Mary. We may be the only ones with an infant.

Most everyone we know has a baby-sitter. There's no nursery here. Besides, it's pretty formal; kids don't really fit in.

We have been on the road. Our clothes are dusty. Our feet hurt. Mary needs a place to lie down.

There's hardly a room that I'd call private. The guests have the run of the house. I don't think we have a place where she can be alone.

We'd rather not be alone; we'd like the people to meet the baby. His name is Jesus. It is his first party. We can sit in a corner anywhere.

Jesus. Sounds foreign. Nobody we know has a name like that. There are Jesus stories, but it's not somebody's real name. The party may go all night.

Mary would give up a night for this, so the people can meet the child.

All parents are proud of their babies. We'll find a place for you. You don't mind that there will be drinking and dancing and music?

We don't mind. Mary understands that the child will know drinking, dancing, singing. The child has a long lineage of music. He comes from the line of David, the king, the dancer and singer.

I'll bring you a glass of wine for a New Year's toast.

We will toast the child. If you like, we will lift up the drink and lead all the guests in a toast to God, for the child.

I didn't plan for this to be a religious night. It's just a big party with hats and horns and fun.

The angel promised the child would grow to make people glad, as some are tonight. Jesus will understand the hugging, the joy, the music.

You really think this kid is special, don't you? You want him to be part of the party.

We want him to be the center, the reason people are glad in the new year. He is new, just born, like a new year, a new time, another chance. He brings us the beginning. That's what a party is about, a new time.

Hmmm. That's true when you think about it.

Tell us when. We will bring the child to show the people. We will toast each other and the child.

You said we would toast God.

That's where God is, in the baby and with us.

All right, let's do it. You can bring Jesus to the top of the stairway. The baby will be our surprise. Just so you know, horns may blow, some people will cheer and hug each other. I'll tell the band to play softly.

Dear God, be the center of our parties.

Battlefield

Hey! You know you're in a danger zone—a war zone? It's barricaded off since the last attack.

The bombing woke the child. We came toward the fire, for the light and warmth. The child has never before seen a battle.

You are bringing a child—a baby—into a war zone? How can you do this?

Joseph and I know that war is all around. Few will escape the tragedy of war. Children, too, must suffer because of war. This child will be seasoned for war, even as an infant.

Watch where you step! We don't know how many children have lost limbs by land mines. This land will never again be filled with happy children, running and playing in the wind.

Show us the pain. Show us where the children suffered. My child must see, too; for he will know war when he is older. His spirit will heal the land.

He will enlist when he is eighteen? You will let him go to war?

When he is two or three years old, a ruler named Herod will send soldiers to hunt him and other children, in order to protect their power and control.

It's all about power, isn't it?

It is all about power. The child Jesus has power of the Most High within him. His power is power for good.

What good can come if you take Jesus to battlefields, to places where children are afraid to play, where children lose their lives?

Children will see a power stronger than that of the Herods who destroy them. They will learn of a Spirit that is stronger than the spirit of greed and ambition and fear, stronger than swords and land mines.

It is growing dark. You will not know where to step in the darkness.

The child will know. We call him Jesus, but he is also known as The Way. He will light the way to peace.

Does this all mean that children of the world will no longer be in wars? That wars will end?

It means that they are never alone; the child Jesus is always with them. And the children will, finally, not be victims. The children will win. There will be peace one day.

You seem so sure, so full of hope.

I believe for sure. This child is a child of peace, the Prince of Peace. I believe in the child. I hope in the child.

Dear God, lead us to peace.

Governor's Mansion

WE NEED A ROOM, WE SAW THE LIGHT.
WILL YOU MAKE US A ROOM FOR JUST TONIGHT?

The governor is with his family. Do you have an appointment?

We wanted to see him before we leave to go home.

It's very late to come to the mansion. You could make a morning appointment.

The baby is awake now. We were nearby. So we decided to see the governor.

I will speak with the governor. He can decide whether to see you or not. Who are you? What names shall I give him?

Tell him Mary is here, and Joseph, and the baby born in Bethlehem.

I recognize those names. We have a manger scene that the governor's wife bought during a trip to Jerusalem. Carved out of olive wood.

We were just near Jerusalem, where we rested under olive trees. The journey was long, and the olive fruit nourished us more than once.

They say olive oil is healthy, that it's good for you.

Olive oil is also used for anointing a king, a queen, maybe even a governor. It is a sign of honor. We have some olive oil with us.

The governor might like that. He likes honor, and he likes his new office. He's just beginning his first term. He has great plans, a wonderful platform.

Jesus, the newborn one, is beginning his term, too. He has plans that were promised by prophets—Amos, Hosea, even Isaiah.

Our governor considers his job a calling. He feels that he, the people, and the office are one. He wears his role of governor as though it were a mantle.

Mary knows a song that he may like. The words are about her child as ruler, but they fit all who govern. All who govern rule under God.

That sounds like a line in our nation's pledge of allegiance: "one nation under God." Every governor, every senator, every leader knows those words.

It sounds like a prayer.

More of a pledge than a prayer, although it takes praying to make it happen.

Do you think we can see the governor tonight?

I think he will see you. Yes, I think he will. Wait here by the crèche, and I will find him. You can look at cards that were sent to him during these holy days. A lot of them mention a woman named Mary and her child Jesus.

We will wait here by the tree with the star on top. When the governor comes, we will give him our gift of olive oil. He can use it on his salad, and he can anoint his brow when he needs courage.

All right, please wait here. I believe the governor will come to see you soon—and perhaps you'll get to meet his whole family. And, by the way, we do have a guest room, just in case you're invited to stay.

Dear God, come to places of power.

House of Stars and Lights

We saw the star in the window. We followed it to your house.

I do not think we've ever met.

I am Mary, this is Joseph, my husband. And this is the child.

The child?

The baby boy, brand-new, is with us. We saw the star in the window and the lights still on the tree.

We don't take our tree down until after Epiphany.

The child is fragile, newborn. We need a night of rest. He will like the lights on your tree. We all like the Christmas decorations.

Christmas is practically over. But if you like decorations, you would have loved the big nativity scene at our church this year—with live people. We don't have grown-ups in our nativity. It's all done by kids. We even had a live baby as Jesus this year. You just missed seeing it.

This child's name is Jesus. He is very lively, wide awake. He is looking at your lights.

The baby in our church didn't even wake. Slept right through it all, and made the director of the play very happy. It was a wonderful crèche: stable, manger, hay, animals—just like the real thing.

My child was born in a humble place like the one you describe—just as the Bible promised. There were animals looking on. And angels. I see you have a small Nativity set here, too.

Yes. We added all kinds of new animals this year: elephants and tigers and monkeys. Our children especially like the animals. Our cat even sleeps there at night. That really makes it all come alive. The baby Jesus is made of Dresden porcelain. Very expensive. We don't ever touch it.

You may hold my child. Joseph and I will sit by your tree with the child, with the plastic elephant and your live cat. Your children can come and hold him, too.

I'll take a photo. That will be a nice gift for our friends. It might be our Christmas card next year.

I know a song they will like. I will sing while they hold the child.

They'll sure like doing that—holding a real live baby. As I said, no one gets to touch the porcelain Jesus we have under the tree. And, please, do stay for the night. We would love to have you as guests. You can take the star with you. A gift for the child.

Thank you. The child will know the stars by heart.

Dear God, this place is also your nativity.

Revival Tent

Welcome. Welcome. Glad to have you join us. It's crowded under the tent. I don't see a single open chair. Could we spread out a blanket here on the grass for you?

Thank you, no. We will stand. Mary wants to take the baby near the front; it is hard to see from here.

You mean she wants the child to see the speaker? The baby looks newborn. The baby will not remember being here or who the speaker was.

Mary wants the speaker to see the child. She believes the speaker will do better when he can glance at the child. The baby is named Jesus Christ.

All the revival speakers use that name a lot. They have studied about Jesus, they talk about Jesus, and that is what the people have come to hear. The air is chilly in here. I hope the child is warm enough.

Mary has wrapped Jesus in swaddling cloth, which keeps the child safe, snug, and warm. And the hearts of people can make a cold place warm. The child will help the speaker to warm the people's hearts.

You don't think going up there will be distracting—I mean, if you get between the speaker and the people, it might distract from the message. What if the baby gets hungry and starts to cry?

Mary will nurse Jesus, then Jesus will be still.

In front of the people? That could distract the speaker and the many people here.

They will find meaning in the nursing. A hungry child wants milk, and when it is fed, it will stop crying and live. That is the Good News the child can bring to the people. The speaker will understand. That is the message he wishes to convey about the Word—the milk of life to the listeners.

You talk like an artist, someone in drama, a filmmaker, a storyteller.

God's Good News is a drama—live theater—a story of what happens in this place and in all the world. The good news is pictures, paintings, songs, a child feeding at his mother's breast.

We have some of those going here, in some way. We have a lot of singing, "Throw Out the Lifeline," "Standin' in the Need of Prayer." We really like "Jesus in the Morning, Jesus at the Noontime, Jesus When the Sun Goes Down." They know those songs by heart.

While they are singing, they can look at the child and the mother. It will remind them of the songs, of the Word. This will be live theater.

Live theater, huh? We're here to hear about Jesus.

Jesus is very much alive in this tent tonight. Just listen to the preacher, and see the faces. And look at this child.

Okay, let's go up close and see if it helps the preaching. Soon they'll be singing many songs by heart.

Then they will want to see the face of the child.

Dear God, show us faces of believers.

Spring and Oak

WE NEED A ROOM, WE SAW THE LIGHT.
WILL YOU MAKE US A ROOM FOR JUST TONIGHT?

We are thirsty. Mary is warm from the long walk. We have not seen much water along the way.

And the child needs his mother's milk. She will want drink for her milk. I know what a new mother needs.

Do you have room for us to stay this night?

You can stay as long as you like—until they come with bulldozers against this oak.

We have been resting in the shade of your tree. It is like a shadow under a wing. But now we need a room.

The oak is sacred to my people. I was born by the tree. I stay by the tree to protect it with my own life. It is sacred. It is a refuge for spirit.

I am Joseph. Mary holds a child who is called Refuge and Strength. The child will learn to know trees. There will be a tree with his name inscribed. He will make a tree sacred. Gabriel said the child is sent by God.

I will hear your story when you have had a drink of water with me, near the oak.

Then you do have a room for us?

First we will drink from the spring near the tree. The earth has given birth to this water. We also will wash our faces and feet. I will bring water to warm later, and we can bathe the child. The water is like a holy place in a journey.

Mary knows a spring in Nazareth. Her mother, Anna, taught her to draw water from a well. She always hears the sound of the deep fountain. The child will be called Water, the Water of Life.

It is a right name for a child. Without water there is always death.

His name is also Jesus. And when he is grown, he will bring life through death on a tree—life that will not end.

For now we stay by the spring and the oak. When we have washed and drunk and the child has fed, we will find a room. A room with an open window, a room beside the water and tree. This night you will hear the water; and if the wind blows, you will hear the leaves move. Our word for wind is "spirit."

This child is of the Spirit. That, too, will be his name: Spirit. And Water.

Now it is time for me to hear your story. Talk about the Child and Water and Spirit.

Thank you, God, for saving us through Water and Spirit.

OTHER CHRISTMAS BOOKS FROM AUGSBURG

The Christmas Bird by Sallie Ketcham
32 pages, illustrated, 0-8066-3871-0

An ancient Christmas legend about courage, kindness, and love beautifully retold for families today.

It Came Upon the Midnight Clear
by Henry F. French
64 pages, illustrated, 0-8066-4050-2

A beautiful retelling of the Christmas story.

Unto Us Is Born by Herbert Brokering
96 pages, 0-8066-43897-4

Thirty-seven reflections for the Christmas season in the form of imaginative dialogues with Mary, the mother of Jesus.